Terry McDonagh

One Summer
in Ireland

Ernst Klett Sprachen
Stuttgart

Terry McDonagh

One Summer in Ireland

1. Auflage   1   7 6 5 4 3 | 2022 21 20 19 18

Nachfolger von 3-12-540016-X
Alle Drucke dieser Auflage sind unverändert und können im Unterricht nebeneinander verwendet werden.
Die letzte Zahl bezeichnet das Jahr des Druckes. Das Werk und seine Teile sind urheberrechtlich geschützt. Jede Nutzung in anderen als den gesetzlich zugelassenen Fällen bedarf der vorherigen schriftlichen Einwilligung des Verlags. Hinweis zu § 52 a UrhG: Weder das Werk noch seine Teile dürfen ohne eine solche Einwilligung eingescannt und in ein Netzwerk eingestellt werden. Dies gilt auch für Intranets von Schulen und sonstigen Bildungseinrichtungen. Fotomechanische oder andere Wiedergabeverfahren nur mit Genehmigung des Verlags.

Layoutkonzeption: Elmar Feuerbach
Illustrationen: Elsie Lennox, London
Gestaltung und Satz: Satzkasten, Stuttgart
Umschlaggestaltung: Elmar Feuerbach
Titelbild: iStock, imagefile / © Peter McCabe
Druck und Bindung: CEWE Stiftung & Co. KGaA, Germering
Printed in Germany

ISBN 978-3-12-540017-7

Contents

Chapter 1

"Time to get up, Carl!"

Carl O'Brien yawned and smiled to himself. It would be his last morning in Hamburg for four weeks. He heard his mother call again: "Get up,
5 lazybones!" The voice still seemed far away.

"Coming."

It was Saturday, still only seven and yet he wasn't grumbling on his way to the shower.

"'Morning, Mum," he said, coming into the
10 kitchen and giving his mother a morning hug.

"If it were only like this every day, Mr O'Brien," she joked.

"Where's Dad?"

"He's still in bed but he'll be down in a minute.
15 He'll want to say goodbye to his special, skinny, dark-haired son."

He loved his Mum and Dad, even if they sometimes had those terrible fights that seemed to go on forever. He was just finishing breakfast when
20 his Dad, Joe, stuck his head round the door.

"So you're off to Ireland today, young man."

"I am, sir."

"Aren't you the lucky man!"

"I am, sir."

25 "You've got your twenty-eight pairs of jeans and socks all neatly folded and packed, I take it?"

"I have, sir."

"You're a genius."

Carl saluted. Joe laughed and sat down to his
30 cornflakes.

---

2 **to yawn** [jɔːn] to open your mouth wide when you are tired – 5 **lazybones** *(informal)* a lazy person – 8 **to grumble** [ˈɡrʌmbl] to complain in a low voice – 8 **shower** [ˈʃaʊə] *Dusche* – 10 **to give s.o. a hug** to put your arms around s.o. – 15 **skinny** *(informal)* very thin – 28 **genius** [ˈdʒiːniəs] very clever person

"And I'm taking my soldier to the airport … Am I glad I don't have to teach at that language school today!"

His mother said she'd go through his things to make sure he hadn't forgotten anything. "But only this time … you're a big boy now … next time you can do it yourself."

"But of course, Mum. You know me."

"I certainly do," she said with a smile.

He could see his parents were sad that he was leaving. He was sad, too, but so excited. He'd see his cousins, Granny and Granddad again. He couldn't wait. He watched for the airport signs as they drove through the streets. His father told him again to be careful, not to talk to strangers, and to double-check his tickets and plane times in Frankfurt.

"Yes, Dad." He was getting annoyed. He'd done this trip so often. *"Mein Gott …* parents! But I'd better keep my mouth shut," he thought.

They parked, Dad carried his bag and he took his small backpack with all his important things in it: passport, tickets, money and, of course, the football magazine. Mum had packed in a book about something or other, but he knew he wouldn't read it. He had to wait for two hours in Frankfurt and he had already planned what he was going to do when he got there. He'd look at the football section in the newspaper shop; he'd sit in a quiet corner, drink coke and read about an kinds of sport; he'd read about the *Bundesliga,* especially HSV – his favourite team.

"Check everything again, Carl," his father shocked him out of his dream world.

"I already have."

---

5 **to make sure** to be certain – 15 **stranger** [ˈstreɪndʒə] person you don't know – 15 **to double-check** to make sure again that s.th. is correct

"Make sure."

He went through his things again. Before Carl knew where he was, they were at the airport and it was time to go to the departure gate. They said
5 goodbye.

"See you in four weeks in Ireland, Carl. Say hello to everybody in Baile Mór and Dublin for me, won't you."

"I will, Dad, I promise," he replied. And with that
10 he went through to his gate and on to his plane for Frankfurt.

Before he knew it, he was arriving in Dublin. Auntie Elaine and his cousin Kate would be at the airport. Kate was one year older but they really
15 liked each other. They lived in Longwood Avenue on the south side – only a fifteen-minute bus ride from the centre. He was so excited.

The door to the Meeting Point opened and he was met by a sea of faces. He very quickly recognized
20 the faces of Elaine and Kate.

4 **departure gate** place where your plane leaves from – 7 **Baile Mór** [bɑːljə muːr] place name (Gaelic for "a big place")

Chapter 2

It was the same Dublin airport, but it seemed different this time – greener somehow and not at all like Hamburg. Ireland was being advertised as a perfect place to go on holidays. It offered rivers,
5 lakes, golf, mountains and rain, he said to himself. He was thinking this as Elaine put her arms around him. Kate stood a little to one side looking cool in her jeans and sweatshirt. She was fifteen. He noticed her black hair was longer and she had
10 grown.

"My goodness, but you've grown, hasn't he, Kate? You and Kate are so similar … you really are."

"Yeah, he has grown, Mum," said Kate. "Typical mother! … and we really look similar … hello,
15 cousin Carl!" She waved at him from about a metre away.

He waved back, too. Elaine shook her head and laughed. "Young people! I must be getting old. Tell me, how is your mother and that big brother of
20 mine in Hamburg?"

She talked so quickly. He realized he'd hardly said a word. She was quite small, slim and energetic with brown hair and lively blue eyes. She was wearing a pair of jeans. His mother never wore jeans.

25 "Great. They send their love. Dad will be home in a few weeks."

Elaine argued about who should take which bag.

"Let me take the big one, you're the visitor," she said.

22 **slim** thin – 27 **to argue** [ˈɑːgjuː] to disagree

"Just because I'm a visitor doesn't mean I'm helpless."

"He's not helpless, Mum," said his cousin. "He's said so himself."

5   Eventually, Elaine took the big bag and he took the small one. Kate was happy to let him, even though her mother protested again, saying he was the visitor and visitors had to be taken care of – for the first few days, anyway.

10   "And, anyway, you have the easy bag, Mum … it's on wheels."

"Kate's cool," he thought.

They made their way to the car park, Elaine leading the way with Carl and Kate coming behind.
15   They liked each other, even if they had little to say at this moment. They put the bags in the car and got in.

"Carl goes in front, Kate."

"I don't mind, I really don't, Kate."

20   "Well, just this time … because you're my cousin." She had a twinkle in her eye and was clever with words. He'd have to learn to think quickly in English to match her.

They got in and Elaine drove the car out into
25   Dublin's traffic.

"Philip will be home early this evening. He promised he would so that we can have dinner together. We'll be passing the shops, so if there's anything you'd really like, please ask."

30   "Can we have sausages, beans and mashed potato?"

---

21 **twinkle** [twɪŋkl] *here:* an expression of fun – 23 **to match s.o.** to be as good as s.o.

"You're easy to please," Kate called out from the back seat.

"Now Kate, if the boy wants sausage, beans and mashed potato on his first evening, he gets sausage,
5 beans and mashed potato."

"I'd love it. We don't have it in exactly the same way in Hamburg."

They took the scenic route, as Elaine called it, and went into the city via Malahide, Portmarnock,
10 Howth Hill, up on the left, and Clontarf. They were all along the sea and it was very nice, he thought. They chatted about school, friends, traffic – all the things you talked about when getting to know one another again.

15 "It's strange being on the left-hand side of the road, and me sitting here. It feels funny. You must come and visit me in Germany, Kate. Then you'll be on the other side."

"It would be brilliant. I'd love to."

20 "Maybe next year, Kate," said her mother. "Money doesn't grow on trees, at least not on our trees."

"I'll get a job, Mum."

"Your school is important, don't forget."

The traffic was very heavy as they crossed the
25 River Liffey. Nobody spoke for a few minutes.

Money had never really been a problem for Carl. His mother was a lawyer and his father taught English. He didn't like his job very much but they never seemed to have money problems. He could
30 have whatever he wanted – not quite, but almost – and still, life was not always so easy.

---

8 **scenic route** a road with beautiful views – 9 **via** ['vaɪə] by way of, through – 12 **to chat** [tʃæt] to talk in an informal and friendly way – 27 **lawyer** *Rechtsanwalt*

"We'll drive up to the house and you and Kate can run round the corner to the shop for your sausages and beans. We have potatoes at home."

"Are we there already?"

5   "Almost," said Kate. "We're on the South Circular Road. It's the next left."

They stopped outside the house, took the bags in and left them in the front room downstairs. They'd take them up after they'd eaten. Elaine gave them
10   some money and they went to the shop.

Chapter 3

These corner shops, as they are called, had a special charm for Carl. They seemed to sell just about everything and were open from early morning until midnight, or later. Kate knew where things were, so
5 they helped themselves.

"That'll be two pounds thirty-five, Kate. How are your Mum and Dad?"

"Great, John, great. Oh, by the way, this is my cousin Carl from Hamburg."

10 "Nice to meet you, Carl. On holidays, are you?"

"That's right."

"Enjoy it."

"Thanks, I will."

Kate paid. They left the shop and walked along the
15 South Circular Road to the second turn left before Longwood Avenue, which took them up to the canal. The canal and the South Circular ran parallel to each other, with streets and houses in between. There was a narrow road between the end houses
20 and the canal, so it was the same distance home from the shop, no matter which way you went.

"It's nicer round the canal way and besides, we have to eat the chocolate before we get home," said Kate.

25 "Your mother said we could buy some."

"Yeah, but not as much as we did."

They walked up the street to the canal and sat on a canal-bank seat. It was about five-thirty. The sun was out but was not very warm. He was glad he had
30 his jacket on. They shared the chocolate and talked about school and friends.

19 **narrow** not very wide – 22 **besides** as well

"Talking of friends, Carl. Here comes Liz, my best friend. She hasn't seen us yet. Hi, Liz!"

"Oh, hi."

"This is Carl. Remember, my cousin I've been telling you about. The guy from Germany."

"Cool."

She didn't sit down, so they stood up and Kate gave her a piece of chocolate.

"Kate and I go to school together. We're in the same class. I live down the street."

Carl thought Liz looked really pretty. She had dark hair and pale skin with a few freckles on her nose. She seemed a bit sad.

"How are things at home, Liz?"

"Oh, the usual. My father's been drinking again. Came home very late last night. I'm so tired of it all."

"Come to our house at about eight and we can listen to some music."

"That's great. I will. Must go. Nice to meet you, Carl."

"See you later, Liz."

"'Bye, Liz," Carl said. People seemed so relaxed with each other.

"Liz is really nice, Kate, isn't she?"

"She's brilliant, she is. And she has such a hard life."

They sat down again and Kate went on to tell him that Liz's mother had died two years ago and her father drank all the time. He used to be very kind – and still was – but he drank far too much and they had very little money.

They got home shortly after six.

"You two took your time. I'll get the food ready. You can take Carl up to his room, Kate."

12 **freckles** little brown spots on the skin from the sun – 30 **kind** [kaɪnd] nice, friendly

"Right, Mum. We met Liz."

"Ah, did you. Poor Liz, with that father and no mother."

They took the bags upstairs to the front room. There were only two rooms, so Carl knew that Kate had to sleep downstairs in the front room while he was with them. He said this to her and she just laughed.

"I don't mind at all. We have a fold-up bed and it's really comfortable."

"Thanks."

"For nothing. It's lovely that you're here."

Philip, Kate's father, was a taxi driver. He was a tall, thin man with a big smile. His hair was still brown, but going grey and thinning on top. Carl wasn't always sure what he was saying. He was a real Dubliner, with a real Dublin accent.

"Slow down, Philip. The lad doesn't know what you're saying," Elaine sometimes said.

"Sorry, son. I forget English is not your language."

By the end of the meal, it was better. Carl loved the sound and melody of this language and he was surprised how well he could speak it himself.

Liz arrived at eight. Elaine gave her tea and cake and the three went to the front room, listened to music and decided to go into the city next day. Liz would come round at eleven.

Carl rang home. All seemed well. His mother was really missing him but he'd see his father in a few weeks. He slept deeply that night.

---

9 **fold-up bed** a bed which you can fold together – 15 **thinning** getting thinner

Chapter 4

Carl woke up. He thought he'd heard a door banging. Within seconds, he knew where he was. Today was going to be a good day. It was Sunday. He looked at his watch – only eight-thirty. He felt it
5 should be later. "Have to go to the toilet." He did. The door of Kate's parents' bedroom was open. "They must be up." He turned on the shower. "Great, it really works!" Not like the one in Baile Mór where his grandparents lived. He had to smile
10 when he thought of it. Their shower seemed to have a life of its own. Carl could not understand why some showers were often broken or did not really work in Ireland. He said this to his father once.

"Goodness, my son's a real German. Everything
15 doesn't have to work perfectly to make people happy."

He knew this was true, but life was easier when things did work – at least in Hamburg. He came out of the shower and went back to his room. It was
20 nine. He heard somebody coming up the stairs.

"'Morning, Carl," Kate shouted. "Did you sleep well?"

"Yes, very well."

"See you in the kitchen when you're ready."

25 He dressed, tidied his room and went down. The kitchen was at the back. It was quite small, but big enough for three or four people to sit at the table. He looked around and saw a picture of Kate's

25 **to dress** to put on your clothes

parents and two children on the wall. He looked long and hard at the boy in the picture. Carl had heard that he had died in an accident, but didn't know exactly how.

5 "That's me, my parents and my brother Tony. He was just four years older than me. My big brother." Kate took him by surprise. He hadn't heard her come in.

"It must have been terrible for you. I can't imagine 10 what it would be like."

"Well, Tony's dead. And he won't come back to us." Tears came to her eyes. "That was his first communion photo."

"What exactly happened, Kate? It was some kind 15 of car accident, wasn't it?"

"A group of joy-riders stole a car and crashed onto the pavement where he was playing. He was only eight years old when he was killed. My mother has gone to church every day since. She's there now. 20 Dad's at work. He says he'll never believe in God again. The joy-riders got away and have never been found."

They ate their cornflakes in silence. They heard the door open. Elaine hung her hat and coat in the 25 hall and came into the kitchen.

"'Morning, Carl. You two must have seen a ghost or something. Is something the matter?"

"We were talking about Tony."

Elaine turned and stared out of the window 30 for a long time. Then she spoke: "I will never forget looking out and seeing the police and the

---

7 **to take s.o. by surprise** to surprise or shock s.o. – 16 **joy-riders** people who steal cars and drive them fast for fun – 17 **pavement** ['peɪvmənt] sidewalk or footpath

ambulance. I wondered what they were doing –
why they were there. I went out to see what was
happening and there was Tony lying dead on the
pavement. I can talk about it now, God rest him. We
5 moved here very shortly afterwards."

"Dad never told me very much about the accident
or if he did, I don't remember."

"You were only three at the time, same age as
Kate."

10 Carl didn't know what to say. He said nothing. It
was Kate who broke the silence. "Liz is coming over
at eleven, Mum. We're going into town."

"Fine, but I'll need your help to hang the curtains
at about four, Kate."

15 "We'll see."

"Carl was glad that they were talking about
something else.

"No *we'll see*. I need you. The curtains have to go
up today. I have no time during the week."

20 "But, Mum."

"No *buts*. Be here at four-thirty at the latest,
please."

"OK. We'll have to rethink the day when Liz
comes. She should be here any moment."

25 "When are you going west, Carl?" asked Elaine.

"Maybe tomorrow, if that's OK."

"Fine. Kate and Philip will take you to Heuston
Station. I'm on night duty at the hospital tonight
and I don't get home until about nine. Your train
30 leaves at eight, I think. I'll check for you and give

---

13 **curtains** [ˈkɜːtnz] *Vorhänge* – 28 **to be on night duty** to work at night

Granny a ring to tell her when you're coming. They'll pick you up in Ballyhaunis."

That ended the discussion on Tony's death. The doorbell rang.

5 "That'll be Liz. Will you open for her, Carl?"

"Sure."

"Hi, Liz, come in."

"Hello, Carl." She smiled warmly and went past him into the kitchen. Elaine and the girls had lots 10 to say to each other. They talked about everyday things and people completely unknown to him, but he didn't feel left out. They were just about to walk out the door when Carl's Mum rang. Elaine talked to her first. Carl told her all was well and that he 15 was missing her. Yes, he was changing his clothes each day and had more than enough socks, T-shirts, underwear and pairs of jeans … "Parents!"

The three of them walked down to the South Circular and got the bus into town. Carl wanted to 20 sit on the upper deck. They had the front seats to themselves.

"This is the life," he thought.

2 **Ballyhaunis** [ˌbɑːlɪˈhɔːnɪs] *Ortsname*

18

Chapter 5

Carl felt really grown-up getting off the bus in the company of two very attractive girls.

"If my friends in Hamburg could see me now. Wow!"

5   They were in Dame Street, right in front of Trinity College. Kate suggested they walk through the university grounds, out the back gate and up to the Burger Bar in Grafton Street.

"Sounds good," Carl said. He had fifty pounds in
10 his pocket, a bank card in his wallet, a Burger Bar up the street and a girl on either side of him. "What more can you ask for?" he thought.

The beautiful old-style buildings and grounds of Trinity were cool, but Grafton Street was a lot
15 cooler. No cars and absolutely packed with young people.

"Where do they all come from?" he asked.

"Mostly Spain, and Italy and some from France," Liz explained. "They spend the summer here
20 learning English."

"And doing other things that make Irish mothers worry," Kate giggled and Liz joined in. They saw Carl was confused.

"Carl needs a little help in understanding these
25 matters, Kate, don't you think?"

Then he understood. "I must be thick," he said to himself. To the others he said: "OK, I give up. If

---

1 **grown-up** like an adult − 15 **packed** (informal) very full − 22 **to giggle** ['gɪgl] to laugh in a silly way − 22 **to join** [dʒɔɪn] **in** to do the same as s.o. else − 26 **thick** (informal) stupid

the Irish girls are anything like you two, these guys don't have a chance."

"I'm nice or haven't you noticed, Carl?"

He had. Liz was playing with him. Her hair, and
5 that simple summer dress she was wearing – he had noticed all right. *"Scheiße!"* He felt his face turning red. The two girls giggled.

"I'm not bad myself," he managed to say, but he felt stupid. Kate rescued him.

10 "Here's the Burger Bar, guys. Let's go in."

Carl could see that Kate was buying for Liz. He would like to have done that but it was too late. Not to make the others feel bad, he bought only one hamburger and one portion of chips for himself. He
15 could have eaten three! They chatted about school, teachers, discos – all the usual things. Outside, the streets were alive with buskers, beggars and young people from Ireland, Italy, Spain, France and many other countries.

20 "I have to be home at four to help my mother," said Kate.

"And what will we do all alone and without her, Carl?" Liz looked at him with a smile in her eyes. She was already fifteen and he was feeling it. But
25 he'd be fifteen in three weeks. He couldn't wait. Kate giggled. These two were always up to something. He hoped he wouldn't blush this time. To his surprise, he saw Liz going a bit red as well.

"We could ask Kate, Liz."

30 It was Kate's turn to feel uncomfortable.

17 **busker** [ˈbʌskə] street musician – 17 **beggar** s.o. who asks for money in the street – 27 **to blush** to turn red in the face

"OK, guys, I give up. I'll go home at half-past three and leave you to yourselves. Right!"

"Right, cousin."

"Brilliant. Just go, Kate, go," said Liz.

5 "Thanks a lot, guys. I know when I'm not wanted."

Carl went to the toilet and on his way back got three large cokes. He felt like a real man, and the girls didn't complain.

10 Time flew. It was one-thirty before they knew it. "Let's go, guys." Kate was on her feet and the others followed down the street to College Green.

"No history or churches, please, girls."

"Don't worry," they both said.

15 "Let's go to Temple Bar," suggested Liz. "It's brilliant, don't you think, Kate? … lots of people go there."

"A great place to take tourists when you can think of nothing else to do."

20 "You're terrible, Kate. I don't want to be your friend any more."

"Your choice, Elizabeth, darling. Let's go to Temple Bar."

They walked through the narrow, busy streets.
25 This used to be a completely run-down area on the south bank of the Liffey. The authorities were going to knock it all down and build new office blocks, until somebody had the clever idea to restore it all.

They walked around enjoying the atmosphere of
30 small shops, restaurants and pubs, without actually going in.

---

25 **run-down** in a very bad condition – 26 **authorities** [ɔːˈθɒrətiz] people in a high position, e.g. the town council – 28 **to restore** [-ˈ-] to repair, to make new again

"It would be nice if some shops stayed open on Sunday in Hamburg," Carl thought to himself.

It was nearly half-past three. Kate began to get ready to go. The sun was out so they sat on the steps on Temple Bar Square where lots of other young people were sitting or just standing and chatting – some were reading.

"Well, I'll be on my way, people. I know you'll miss me terribly."

"Kate, I'll never be your friend again, never, if you don't shut up."

"Good. Oh, by the way, Carl, try to be home before eight. We can't have our young people running about late at night now, can we?"

"Just go, Kate."

"As I said, I'm on my way, Liz, darling."

"See you at seven-fifty-nine, Kate," Carl said. He knew it wasn't very funny, but he tried.

Carl and Liz stood alone in Temple Bar.

"By the way, I'm Elizabeth Mary Joyce."

"I'm Carl Damien O'Brien."

She took his hand for a moment. They both blushed.

Chapter 6

They stood there, uncomfortable in each other's company. Liz broke the silence: "Let me show you around."

"Great, where should we go?"

5 "I know some nice clothes and record shops across the river on the north side. Even if they're not open, we can look at the windows. What do you think?"

"It's your city. You can show me around. If you 10 come to Hamburg, I'll show you my city."

"The north side is poorer than the south side, but it's more fun. Let's go."

They came through Merchant's Arch to Merchant's Quay. The traffic lights were red, but 15 nobody seemed to care. They crossed between the cars. Carl was a little nervous about crossing in this way. In Hamburg, he'd have waited.

"Come on," Liz grabbed him by the hand. They crossed the road to a narrow footbridge over the 20 river. "The Ha'penny Bridge. We have to make a wish on it on the way back."

Everything in Dublin seemed to be a bit untidy. When he looked at the state of some of the electric cables he was shocked.

25 "In Germany, you'd be put in prison for that," he thought to himself.

They walked through many small streets on the north side of the river: Capel Street, Mary Street,

14 **quay** [kiː] – 18 **to grab** to take quickly – 20 **ha'penny** [ˈheɪpnɪ] half penny, *here:* name of a bridge

Abbey Street and many others. They went in and out of a few open shops without buying anything: it was lovely just looking and being together. Eventually, they came into O'Connell Street near
5 the General Post Office.

"People call it the GPO," Liz told him.

"Is this where all the fighting took place on Easter Sunday, 1916?" Carl asked.

"How do you know that?"

10 "From Dad."

"You know more than I do."

"My Dad isn't very happy in Germany. He keeps talking about Ireland ... I don't think he's ever really left it."

15 "Why's that?"

"Don't know. It just is."

"You know, your English is fantastic, Carl. How did you learn it?"

"At home and in school. English is very important
20 for us in Germany."

"I do French at school but I can't put a sentence together ... should be ashamed of myself, I should. Most of the others are no better."

"If you have English as your first language, you
25 can go everywhere. Maybe other languages don't seem as important to you."

Liz nodded. "I suppose so." They walked on in silence. "You know, when we get to the Ha'penny Bridge, we have to throw a coin into the water and
30 make a wish. You don't have to tell me what your wish is, but it must be special."

22 **to be ashamed** [əˈʃeɪmd] **of oneself** *sich schämen*

"OK, I promise." He felt nervous. It was four-thirty already. He couldn't believe it. Back on the bridge they faced west. They were silent for a while.

Then Liz said suddenly, "I hate home. My
5 mother's dead. She died two years ago. My father is a nice man, but he's an alcoholic. The little money I earn after school working in a shop goes on food. If only I had a brother or sister, it would at least be something."
10 "Kate told me ... and I sometimes think I've got problems."

"I don't know what I'd do without Kate and her mother."

"We have enough money at home, but my parents
15 don't get on. I've often wished they'd separate." He had tears in his eyes. Liz took two single pennies out of her pocket. She gave one to Carl.

"Hold this coin in your right hand. Give me your other hand and I'll hold my penny in my left hand."
20 They held hands, closed their eyes and made a wish before throwing their coins into the dark and dirty River Liffey. Liz grinned, let go of his hand and began to run to the end of the bridge. He followed happily. The lights were green, so they
25 kept running until they were back where they'd started. He bought two cokes and they sipped them while walking along the cobblestone streets. There were tourists everywhere; Irish traditional music was being played live in one pub – they went in
30 and listened for a while. Then they went round to Meeting House Square where a market was just

7 **to earn** [ɜːn] to get money for work – 26 **to sip** to drink slowly, in small mouthfuls –
27 **cobblestone** square stones used to make old streets

finishing. Some arty-looking people and a few others like themselves walked about as if trying to slow down time.

"We could go up to Dublin Castle. The grounds
5 are really nice. It's only round the corner."

"Lead the way."

They went past the Project Arts Centre, the back entrance of the Clarence Hotel and turned left into Parliament Street. The Castle was up in front. He
10 noticed a pizza menu on the wall of a restaurant across from the Castle as they walked past. Walking was hungry work. The Castle grounds were lovely but he was dying for a pizza.

"Would you let me buy you a pizza, Liz?" he said
15 suddenly.

"You must be crazy. It costs a fortune. If I eat, I pay. Sorry, Carl."

"Please. I'd love to. What's money anyway?"

"A lot, when you've got none."

20 After a five-minute argument she gave in – and even admitted she was hungry. They went in and got a table by the window. At the beginning, it was strange being together in a restaurant. But there was so much to talk about and the time went fast.
25 He'd spend a few days in Dublin before he went back home to Hamburg, he decided.

"That's great news, Carl! Fantastic!"

"Dublin's fabulous," he said to himself.

Before they knew it, it was seven-thirty. They paid
30 and set off on foot for the South Circular. "That's a big church, Liz. What is it?"

"Saint Patrick's Cathedral. A famous writer called Jonathan Swift used to be vicar, or whatever

---

1 **arty-looking** looking like an artist or a writer – 13 **to be dying for s.th.** *here:* to really want s.th. badly – 16 **fortune** ['fɔːtʃuːn] *here:* a lot of money – 30 **to set off** to leave; to start out for a place – 33 **vicar** priest of the Church of England or Ireland

Protestants call their priests. He wrote that book, *Gulliver's Travels*. To be honest, I'm not sure when he lived."

"Doesn't matter." On the last part of their journey they were silent. He walked her to her door.

"I can't ask you in," said Liz quickly. "Thanks for a brilliant day. I cannot kiss you now, either. The neighbours are watching behind the curtains. Thanks again." She blew him a kiss. Carl blushed. She laughed. "Remember, I'll buy the pizza next time."

"Don't worry, I won't forget. See you in three weeks." He turned and headed for Kate's house. He'd got to love the sound of the word *brilliant.*

Perfect. It was just before eight as he rang the bell.

"How was your evening, cool dude?" It was Kate who opened the door. He wished so, so much that he could speak English like the native speakers.

"If only this were in German," he thought to himself. "Great. Really good," he said aloud.

Kate stood waiting for more. "So that was it … *great, really good.* Well, if you continue to be as tight-lipped as you are at present, I'll just have to question my best friend Liz after you've gone. Come in, young man."

"Thank you ever so much, lady of the house."

It was fun with Kate. Her parents were sitting at the kitchen table drinking tea. Before they had a chance to open their mouths, Kate said again: "I'm disappointed, I really am. My cousin spends the afternoon with my best friend in the city and I am not informed of the details."

---

1 **priest** *katholischer Pfarrer* – 2 **to be honest** to tell the truth – 16 **cool dude** *(AE)* stylish man about town – 23 **to be tight-lipped** to say nothing, to be quiet

"Leave the poor lad alone, Kate."

"I won't, Mum, not until he comes up with the truth, the whole truth and nothing but the truth."

"I had a great day. I think I know Dublin very well already."

"I'll check with Liz."

"Enough, enough, Kate. Get the lad a drink and something to eat. He must be starving. Sit down there and eat up. Don't listen to that daughter of mine, if you've any sense," Elaine was laughing as she spoke.

"Thanks a lot, Mother."

"I can't eat a thing. I've had far too much to eat today."

"Are you sure, Carl? You're not just saying that to be polite, I hope!"

"Mum, don't try to make him eat if he doesn't want to. He'll have to go on a diet to please his new love." She was really enjoying herself. They all laughed – even Carl, who was feeling just a little bit embarrassed.

The evening went on in this fun way. Philip read the paper, Elaine went to work at nine-thirty and Carl went to bed at ten. Before she went, Elaine made him promise he'd spend a few days with them on his way home to Germany. Carl had planned to do this anyway, but he was pleased she had asked.

"I'll wake you at six-thirty, Carl."

"Thanks, Uncle Philip."

"'Night, cousin."

"'Night, Kate. See you in the morning."

---

8 **to be starving** *here:* to be very hungry – 18 **to go on a diet** ['daɪət] to eat less in order to get thinner – 21 **to be embarrassed** [-'--] to feel uncomfortable in a situation

Chapter 7

Carl was on the train to Westport before he woke up properly. Kate and Philip had taken him to the station and made sure he got on.

"Don't forget, you get off at Ballyhaunis."

5   "He's not thick, Daddy."

They waved to each other as the train pulled out. A new journey was beginning.

Three hours later, Carl collected his bags to alight from the train in the small town of Ballyhaunis, 10 County Mayo. He'd seen wonderful racehorses on the flat, rich land of County Kildare and he'd crossed the river Shannon at Athlone. Time had flown. People had smiled a lot at him and he was surprised how easy it was to talk to people, if you 15 wanted to.

The train stopped at Ballyhaunis station. He saw his relatives before they could see him. Then they saw him and ran to meet him. Auntie Peggy, Elaine's and Dad's sister, Granddad and Martina, his 20 thirteen-year-old cousin, were really pleased to see 'the young German', as his grandfather sometimes called him. Peggy, Elaine and his Dad looked very similar but his father's hair was darker.

Granddad took his bag. Even though his hair was 25 white and he was quite old, he, too, was full of life.

"Let's get into the car first, Peggy, before we begin with questions," he said. "Let me take a look at you. You're more like your mother than your Dad. You've got her eyes. Don't you think so, Peggy?"

---

8 **to alight** [-'-] **from s.th.** to get off s.th. , e.g. a train

"Leave the lad alone, Dad. He hasn't been on the platform for two minutes and you see Katrin's eyes. Say hello to your cousin, Martina. You're a nice one. Carl comes all the way from Germany to visit us
5 and you hardly say hello."

They were in the car and on the way to Baile Mór within five minutes. Ballyhaunis was a small place of about five or six hundred people, but they called it a town – Baile Mór wasn't much bigger. In Germany,
10 they'd be small villages. They went through Knock – the Blessed Virgin Mary was supposed to have been seen by a number of people at the church wall over a hundred years ago, and since then, hundreds of visitors have come to Knock daily.

15 In Baile Mór things became more familiar to him. The chip shop was still there, he noticed happily. He saw, too, Shane Kelly's bike outside the door of his house. Shane was his best friend in the area. They didn't stop, but drove on through the village and
20 down the little side road to where his grandparents lived. He would be staying with them. His eighteen-year-old cousin Dan and his Uncle Brendan would come to visit later in the evening.

"Well, here we are, my boy."

25 Granny was on the doorstep waiting to greet him. He saw all the flowers and small trees and the white house. All the rich smells and the silence. She took him in her arms: "My goodness, but you're the big boy. You must be starving. Lunch is almost ready."

30 "What's for lunch, Granny?"

"Guess."

11 **the Blessed Virgin** [ˈvɜːdʒɪn] **Mary** the mother of Jesus – 15 **to be familiar** [fəˈmɪljə] **with s.th.** to know s.th. well – 25 **to greet** to say hello, to welcome

"Shepherd's pie?"

"Correct!"

"Brilliant."

"I wish I was the German cousin," Martina laughed.

"Now, now, child. I see you every day. Come on, let's go in."

"We won't be staying," Peggy said. "I have to get lunch for the men. Come on, Martina. See you later, Carl."

It was a fresh, sunny day in July.

---

1 **shepherd's** [ˈʃepedz] **pie** a dish of mince with mashed potato on top

Chapter 8

A week went by. In Mayo, things were more relaxed than they had been in Dublin. Carl stood in his bedroom on the first floor, and looked out of the window to the nearby hills. He had been for a
5 walk through these hills almost daily, alone or with his grandfather. He'd been to Castlebar with Uncle Brendan for items for the farm or in his small bus driving people to different places and events. Brendan explained that he couldn't live
10 from farming alone. Most of his runs were to take old people shopping, or young people to pubs and discos. Sometimes Martina came as well, although she was usually shy and spent most of her time with
15 her own friends. Dan, who wanted to become a vet, would be going to Dublin in autumn to begin his studies. New information was coming at Carl from all sides.

His friend Shane came to visit as often as he could and they cycled the many narrow roads that
20 seemed to lead nowhere. They sometimes took off their shoes and tried to catch little fish in the streams. They loved going to the old graveyard and to some old, empty houses where they could feel a certain sense of fear – and they even cut their
25 names into the bark of old trees.

Shane, who played on the under-sixteen Gaelic football team, was having a game on the coming Sunday. Carl asked if he could join in the training.

4 **nearby** ['nɪəbaɪ] which are near – 10 **run** *here:* bus journey – 14 **shy** [ʃaɪ] nervous in the company of other people – 22 **graveyard** place where dead people lie – 25 **bark** the skin of a tree – 26 **Gaelic** ['geɪlɪk] **football** *(see p. 57)*

On his first evening, a really tough-looking boy called Tom asked him who he was.

"Carl. I'm Carl O'Brien."

"Where are you from?"

5 "Hamburg."

"Hamburg! Where's Hamburg?"

"Germany."

"Say something in German."

He did and was accepted as someone who spoke 10 another language and might be good enough at Gaelic football. Dad had taught him the rules and they had always got videos of the important matches from home. Home was always Ireland for his father – never Hamburg.

15 His cousin Dan was eighteen and a wonderful footballer. He played midfield on the senior team and had played for the county under-eighteens. He had even played in Croke Park – the big stadium with seventy thousand seats in Dublin. Carl and 20 Shane went to see him play a club match against Claremorris. Dan was the best man on the team. He moved so well with the ball and was always in position to take a pass. Baile Mór won. It was really exciting near the end. There were only three 25 minutes left to play. Then Dan caught a high ball, turned and kicked the ball over the crossbar to score a beautiful point. With ten seconds to go, they got a goal and the crowd went wild – they had won a very important match.

30 Dan looked so much like Brendan, his father. They were both tall and dark and quiet, and they

9 **to accept** [ək'sept] **s.o.** to welcome s.o. (in a group) – 17 **county** ['kaʊnti] Grafschaft – 26 **crossbar** top part of a goal post *(see p. 58)* – 27 **to score** to get a goal or a point in a game

did everything they could to make Carl feel at home. When the game was over, they all went to the pub to celebrate. Carl and Shane had coke. The adults had glasses of beer and Guinness. The
5 place was full of kids, mothers, sisters, players and husbands – someone even sang a song. Dan was with the team, but he came over to Carl to make sure he had something to drink. A number of the under-sixteens were playing pool billiards in the
10 corner. When the table was free, Carl had a game with Shane, which he lost.

Brendan and Dan were just getting into the car when they saw Carl and Shane leaving.

"Leave the bike with Shane and come to us for
15 tea, Carl," Dan called.

"I'd love to, Dan, if that's OK with you, Shane?"

"No problem. I'll take care of the bike. Don't forget training tomorrow night."

"I'll be there. See you."

20 At Dan's they had fried bacon, eggs, sausage and chips for tea – Carl thought he was going to burst. Afterwards, he watched TV with Martina for a while. Brendan and Dan read the papers and Peggy went to visit a friend.

25 Carl could have walked through the fields to his grandparents' house, but he had to admit he was afraid of the bulls, as he called them. Martina, who was usually quiet, giggled and, finally, started laughing:

30 "They're harmless, Carl!"
He felt stupid.

---

21 **to burst** [bɜːst] to break open suddenly when full – 27 **bull** [bʊl] male animal of the cow family – 28 **finally** ['faɪnəli] in the end – 30 **harmless** not dangerous

"I'll take you over in the car, Carl," said Brendan. "I've got something to do on the way anyway. Don't laugh, Martina. You wouldn't do very well in Hamburg on your own, young lady, now would
5 you?"

"I know that, but how could anybody be afraid of our cattle?"

Even Carl began to see the funny side of it himself.

10 His Dad would be coming soon. He'd ring him and Mum from Granny's.

4 **on your own** alone

Chapter 9

Granny and Granddad were quite old. He wasn't sure how old – it wasn't something you asked in Ireland. In Germany, you could ask and you'd get an answer but in Ireland, you just didn't ask. They were
5 still fit and healthy. He always heard them getting up and going down the stairs at about eight each morning. He was called at nine, came downstairs to the bathroom and was at the breakfast table at nine-thirty.

10 "We've always done it this way, haven't we, Michael?"

"Yes, I suppose we have, Mary."

"When you were teaching and the kids were at school, we used to be earlier but we always had
15 breakfast together."

"True. True enough. We did. My goodness, how time flies. It seems like only yesterday since your Dad and the others were kids, Carl."

Granny was quite round, and with her grey hair
20 tied back in a bun and her long jacket, she looked like an old lady on a postcard. They had a very old car in which they drove to town after breakfast to do the shopping and talk to friends.

"It gets us out of the house for an hour."

25 Granddad had lots of books in the living room and he always read for a while in the afternoons or evenings. He loved to talk about his time as a teacher, and tell tales of the fairies and the magic

---

20 **bun** *here: Dutt* – 28 **fairy** a little creature that people imagine *(Fee)* – 28 **magic** [ˈmædʒɪk] special power that can make impossible things happen

in the hills. He had a way of telling tales that made Carl want to listen. This year the stories meant even more to him. Perhaps it was because he was growing up and really wanted to learn about his
5 family history. When the afternoons or evenings were fine, they walked up the hills together and stood looking around, or sat on fallen trees or large stones while they talked.

"See where you're standing, Carl. What do you
10 see?"

"I'm standing on a mound. It's circular, about fifty metres across. It's called a ring fort."

"Excellent. I couldn't have described it better myself."

15 "I'm just repeating what you told me before we came up."

"I forgot. Old age is terrible," he laughed. "A long time ago, families lived in the larger forts. The smaller ones could have been places where children
20 were buried. It is said that 'the little people' – as fairies are sometimes called – now live there. These places must not be touched, and even trees on or near a ring fort may not be cut down."

"Why not?"

25 "It could bring bad luck."

"You're joking?"

"No, I'm not. There are many examples of people who cut down fairy trees and had bad luck afterwards."

30 "What, for example?"

"The cattle died or cows did not give milk."

---

11 **mound** small hill – 11 **circular** [ˈsɜːkjʊlə] round – 12 **ring fort** place where people used to live a long time ago – 20 **to bury** [ˈberi] to put s.th., e.g. a dead person, in the ground – 25 **bad luck** unhappiness

"But how do you know which is a fairy tree?"

"A tree standing alone in the middle of a field could be one. It is said they are meeting places for 'the little people'. Take that old blackthorn bush
5 over there, for example."

Carl walked over and looked hard at the old bush. Then he turned and came back to where his grandfather was still standing.

"Have you ever seen a fairy, Granddad?"
10 "Not personally, but I knew a man – he's dead now – who saw a fairy funeral at midnight on the road through the woods. He told me himself how, from a safe distance, he'd watched them carry the tiny coffin down to the old graveyard by the river."
15 "You mean, near where we went fishing?"

"Yes, that's it. The old man had seen this as a boy and had never forgotten it, and he didn't ever tell anyone where it was. Some say the fairies made him promise to keep it secret; we'll never know.
20 Why was he the only one to have seen it? Was he a chosen one? Much later, a local poet wrote a poem about the story."

"Could I read it?"

"I can tell it to you. Would you like to hear it?"
25 "I'd love to."

---

4 **blackthorn** *Schwarzdorn* – 11 **funeral** ['fjuːnərl] *Begräbnis* – 14 **tiny** ['taɪni] very small – 14 **coffin** wooden box for a dead person – 21 **chosen** ['tʃəʊzn] **one** a very special person

The Fairy Funeral

In stillness at midnight
fairies carried their tiny coffin
through an old hole
5 *in a forest fence.*

Their weeping was quiet
on the road, but a child
heard it and followed
to their secret graveyard.

10 *They knew he'd been sent*
by the old storyteller
and that gave them joy.

It wasn't easy to understand. Later that evening, he got his Granddad to write it down. Next night, 15 they took the path the fairies had walked to the graveyard.

"When I stand here, I think of Elaine's beautiful son." There were tears in his eyes. "He was a thoughtful boy, like you, Carl. He would have 20 understood." He put his hand on Carl's shoulder.

On that night in that graveyard, Carl O'Brien felt he understood a little of the mystery of life and of the wisdom of old age.

23 **wisdom of old age** *Weisheit des Alters*

Chapter 10

Time passed very quickly. Carl was to spend four weeks in Ireland. He was into his third week and still enjoying it. He cycled to Baile Mór when he felt like it, sent cards to his mother and friends in
5 Hamburg and bought little presents to take back with him. He liked to be alone when doing these things. Dad would be coming next week. He'd hire a car in Dublin and drive over to the West. They'd do a lot together. He and Martina understood each
10 other much better now, but he still felt silly when he thought about those harmless cattle. Now he wasn't afraid of them at all.

He'd been to Castlebar, Swinford, Foxford and to many other places with Brendan in the bus. His
15 Granny fed him well and he played football in the town park with Shane and the team. He improved very quickly – so much so that he was asked if he'd like to play in a friendly match against Ballyhaunis on the following Wednesday evening.
20 "My father will be here to see me," he thought. He was so happy.

He took the ball with him wherever he went. He kicked it at walls, ran through the fields trying to pick it up with his foot without bending down, and
25 he practised solo-runs – kicking the ball from his foot to his hand while running and without letting it fall. Shane was really skilful, as was Dan, who gave him lots of very useful tips. Carl didn't want

27 **skilful** very good at s.th.

the others in the team to see that he hadn't played as much as them, so he worked harder than most during their training.

Even though they lost last Sunday's game in the end, Shane had scored a goal and three points. Carl watched every move: how he turned, kicked or ran with the ball – people were saying he could be a county player one day. He was really fast, and he could lift the ball up so easily with his toe. Their fathers had played together as young men.

"Your Dad was a tough player, I'll say that for him," said one man to him after training. Carl wasn't quite sure what that meant and didn't ask. People had begun to ask when they realised who Carl was: "How's your father?"

"Very well, thank you," Carl always said politely.

"Tell him, I said hello."

"He'll be home next week."

"That's good news. We're sure to meet him in town."

Carl had no idea who these people were, but it didn't matter.

"A grand man … a grand man altogether … and a tough man on the football field, I'll say that for him."

"Come on, Carl. Can't you see, he's had a few beers too many," whispered Shane. Carl smiled and they walked away happily.

"You played a fantastic game, Shane."

23 **grand** great

"Not bad, I suppose, but I hate losing. Remember, it's your turn next Wednesday. Let's talk in the chip shop."

They sat with about half the team. Carl really felt that he was a member of the group.

"You know what these Ballyhaunis guys are like, Carl?" the captain said.

"Not really, Tom. I've never played a full game here."

"They're tough. They don't know you, so they'll hit hard to test you. Don't worry, we'll be waiting for dirty tricks. You just play the ball. OK, lads?"

"Carl's our man!" came from the corner and they all cheered and chanted, "Carl's our man!"

They talked in this easy way for about an hour. Then they went home in ones, twos and threes.

He hoped he'd play well in front of his father – maybe even score a point. The size of the field, the number of players and the rules kept going through his head. He knew the rules very well – he'd seen the game often enough but it was another thing to play with people who'd played the game all their lives. They didn't have to think – he did. If it was a game of soccer, he could have shown them a thing or two.

Liz was often on his mind as well. He'd like to have sent her a card, but he didn't dare. He'd see her soon anyway.

27 **to dare** to be brave enough to do s.th. dangerous

Chapter 11

They had just finished breakfast when a car stopped outside.

"Now, I wonder who that could be at this early hour, Michael," said Carl's grandmother.

5 "I don't know, Mary," said his grandfather, getting up and going to the window to look out. But before he'd got to the window, the back door opened and Carl's father walked in.

"Dad!" cried Carl and ran into his arms.

10 "Let me see how they've been treating you, my son. Not bad by the look of things."

Joe went to his mother and father and hugged them in turn. They were so happy to see him and he to see them.

15 "I got in yesterday evening, hired a car and stayed the night with Elaine and the gang in Dublin. What have I been hearing about you, young man? All alone with a young lady in the big city of Dublin!"

Granny and Granddad looked at each other 20 knowingly.

"He's like his father used to be, isn't he, Mary?"

"He certainly is, Michael."

They all laughed, but Carl was glad when they started talking about something else.

25 "Is Katrin well, Joe?" Granny sounded worried.

"She's fine, really. She'll phone you for your birthday on Wednesday, Carl."

"On Wednesday? Oh … but I won't be here."

"Why not? Where are you going?"

30 "You won't believe it, Dad. I'm playing for the Baile Mór under-sixteen team in a friendly match on Wednesday. "

"You're what? I can't believe it – my son playing for Baile Mór."

"It's true, Joe," said Granddad. "My grandson is playing Gaelic football, and is very good, from all I
5 hear."

"I can't believe it. I just can't believe it."

"You'll have a cup of tea, Joe?"

"I'm dying for one, Mum."

Carl's grandmother poured the tea and then the
10 grandparents left the room to give them some time together. Joe and Carl were so pleased to see each other. They talked and talked about this and that and things that had happened in Hamburg as well as in Mayo.

15 "Listen, Carl. I'm very tired. I had a late night last night and I've been driving since early morning, so I feel like a nap. I'll be up again in three hours. You tell Peggy, Brendan and anyone else you see, that we're going to the pub tonight. I need a few beers
20 and some good laughs. After we've celebrated your birthday and your match on Wednesday, you and I are off for a few days together. How about that, son?"

"Brilliant, Dad."

25 "Brilliant? Where did you learn that?"

"A little bird whispered it in my ear."

"I'm going to bed. I don't recognise my own son any more. The world has gone mad. See you, man," said Joe and went to bed.

30 Granny and Granddad came back in to talk to him.

"You're more like your mother, Carl, isn't he Mary?"

"Exactly like her, if you ask me," answered Granny.

9 **to pour** [pɔː] to put tea, etc. in a cup – 17 **nap** short sleep during the day

"The same nose, dark hair and eyes. A lovely lady your mother, a lovely lady."

"We haven't seen her for a few years," said Granddad. "Maybe next year. It would be nice to see her again."

"Mum's very busy at the moment," explained Carl. "She said she'd have a week in Spain … needed the sun, she said."

All three were silent for a few minutes.

"Is it OK if I call Mum? I'd just like to tell her Dad has arrived safely."

"You don't have to ask, Carl. Give her our love." His mother sounded happy. She said she'd be in Spain for the next week but she'd call him on Wednesday. And she'd be at the airport with a big hug to meet him. She missed her little man so much. She promised she'd come next year to visit. She'd love to see them all, too.

The pub was not quite Carl's thing, but he enjoyed it just the same. They all went, even his grandparents. The young people sat together, as did the adults at another table. Granddad liked his little whiskey, Granny her glass of port and the others had glasses of beer or Guinness. Martina and Carl got coke and crisps. She told him of the new disco that was being built and about a guy she fancied in her class at school. He didn't dare tell her about Liz, even though he'd have liked to. Shane was the only person he'd told. Dan was at the pub, too, and gave him lots of tips for Wednesday.

"It's the day after tomorrow. Wow!" he thought. His birthday was not so important this year. Anyway, birthdays didn't seem to be as important as they were in Germany, he told himself. Friends

23 **port** a sweet wine – 26 **to fancy** |ˈfænsi| **s.o.** to like s.o. very much, to find s.o. attractive

of Dan's sat with them and he talked to them for a while. Then Shane and his father arrived.

"Shane's my very best friend," he thought.

He heard his father say, "I can't believe it … my son playing for Baile Mór." The conversation went on and on. Some more drinks arrived. People were coming over to his Dad all the time to welcome him home.

"Can I get you a drink, Joe?"

"No, please, no! I must have about three coming up, Seamus."

"Great to see you again. Maybe you might come to the game next Sunday. We need someone to carry the jerseys."

They all laughed.

Joe seemed very happy, much happier than he'd been in Hamburg. One thing Carl was beginning to realize was that his father was a great talker and storyteller.

At ten-thirty, Granddad and Granny stood up. "It's fine for you young people, but some of us have to get up in the morning. Mary and myself will be getting on our way. We'll take Carl with us, Joe."

Joe went to Carl and put his arm round him. "See you in the morning, son. Goodnight."

"Night, Dad."

Peggy began to pick up her things, too. "Well, Martina, I think it's time we went as well. Brendan has an early run. I suppose we won't see you for a few hours, Dan."

"Correct, Mother."

The little group went out into the damp Irish night. The voices the others could be heard through the open window.

---

11 **Seamus** [ˈʃeɪməs] a friend of Joe's (Gaelic for "James") – 14 **jersey** [ˈdʒɜːzi] football shirt

Chapter 12

"It's brilliant having Dad here," Carl was thinking as he got dressed on the morning of his birthday, and of the game. Just as he was coming down the stairs, the phone rang. Dad picked up the phone.

"Oh, it's you, Katrin. He's on his way." They spoke for a few minutes.

"They are having a laugh together," Carl thought as he took the phone. Mum was in great form. She missed him so much, but she'd see him in a week. In Spain the weather was just wonderful. She and Dad had a big birthday surprise waiting for him when he got back.

"Ask Dad. Maybe he'll tell you."

"Oh, Mum."

"Ask Dad."

She was laughing more than she had laughed for months. In the end, Joe told him: "We got you that bike you wanted, Carl."

"Fantastic, Dad!"

He was walking on air. Brendan was away in his bus, but Peggy, Dan and Martina came by with cards, twenty pounds and best wishes. There were cards from Mum, Elaine, Kate and Philip, and one from Liz. He put her card into his pocket and read it again and again, when he was alone. She was looking forward to seeing him. Brilliant!

Granny and Granddad gave him a beautiful copy of *The Fairy Funeral.* He would have it for the rest of his life.

Shane arrived with *The Rules of Gaelic Football[1]*
5 "Hope I'm not too late, Carl." He smiled at his friend.

"Better late than never. Thanks, Shane. I'll have to score at least one point this evening. Hope it doesn't rain."

10 "We'll win anyway. See you at half-past seven. Take it easy."

The others left, and they had lunch. Afterwards, the old folk went for a nap. Carl and Dad went up the hills for a walk – they had to talk about tactics
15 for the match.

They were at the pitch at seven-thirty. Brendan, Dan and Martina arrived just as the ball was being thrown in at eight. Carl was playing in the attack, on the left wing. The first ball that came to him, he
20 lost. He was angry with himself. Shane ran over to him and told him not to worry. The next ball he got, he passed to Shane, who put it over the bar for a point. At half-time, Ballyhaunis were leading by one goal and five points to one goal and three points.
25 He'd got the ball a few times; he had even taken a shot at goal, but he missed. One guy hit him on the back of his head when the referee wasn't looking – it really hurt.

"That's the last time you'll try that with me,
30 mister," he thought. But all in all, he was pleased

1 see p. 57

13 **folk** [fəʊk] people

with the game. Jack, the coach, spoke to him and asked him to move to Baile Mór.

"We could do with a few more like you, Carl. I saw that little incident. You've got a lot of your old man in you and you are better with the ball."

His father and the small crowd cheered every time he went near the ball. He could hear lots of instructions but he ignored them and played his own game.

"If only I could get a score," he heard himself say as the second half began. Ten minutes into the game, Tom played a high ball to him. He ran, jumped, caught it cleanly, turned and kicked the ball high into the air and over the bar.

"I've done it! This is the happiest day of my life!" He looked over to his Dad. They would never forget this moment. There was cheering on and off the field. It was all a dream. They won the game by three points. Carl scored another and gave Shane the pass for the last score of the game.

Later at home, each of his moves was lived through again and again in great detail. Carl even told his father what the coach had said.

"Did he now? You can't believe everything people tell you and, anyway, if you are half as good as I was, you'll be all right. But remember, we're off on our trip tomorrow – even stars need some sleep."

Carl slept well and had wonderful dreams.

---

4 **incident** [ˈɪnsɪdənt] s.th. unpleasant that happens – 8 **to ignore s.th.** to pretend that you don't hear or see s.th.

Chapter 13

They set off at eleven o'clock to be in Westport for lunch. It was only about an hour's drive, but they didn't want to hurry. The day was very mixed, no rain but no sun either. Their aim was to climb
5 the mountain Croagh Patrick sometime in the afternoon. Saint Patrick, Ireland's patron saint, had brought Christianity to Ireland in the fifth century and he was supposed to have fasted for forty days and nights on this mountain – therefore the name.
10 They parked in the town and walked around for a while. There were tourists everywhere.

"If you want to speak German, you'll have no problem here, Carl," laughed Joe.

It was strange hearing his language being spoken
15 on the streets of Westport. The town itself was beautiful and very modern. Joe showed Carl Matt Molloy's pub. Carl had seen Matt Molloy play the flute with the "Chieftains" in the *Stadtpark* in Hamburg. They looked in, but the great man
20 himself wasn't there.

"Westport's one of the few planned towns in Ireland," Joe explained.

"How do you mean, planned?"

"As you can see, it's built on a hill beside the sea.
25 Well, it didn't just happen that way, people sat down and planned how the town should look and where it should be built."

---

5 **Croagh** [krəʊk] – 6 **patron** [ˈpeɪtrən] **saint** *Schutzpatron* – 8 **to fast** to have no food or drink for some time

"Oh, I see. Look, Dad, the clouds are going away. Is that the mountain over there?"

"Yes, it is. Hope you're not getting nervous. We're going up there in about two hours. It's not very high, less than eight hundred metres above sea level, but it looks great, doesn't it?"

"I can't wait. Let's get something to eat first, I'm hungry."

Carl had a big burger with lots of chips and his father had fish. Afterwards, they drove out to Murrisk, the small village at the foot of Croagh Patrick on Clew Bay.

The sun came out, and the air was very fresh. You could see a few people on the small path that seemed to lead up through the clouds into the skies – they looked tiny near the top.

"Let's go, kid."

"OK, boss."

The first part of the climb was easy, but the last part was very steep and they kept slipping on the loose stones. They got to the top after about an hour.

"Look Dad, a small church!"

"Yes, on the last Sunday in June – it's called Reek Sunday – thousands of people climb up here, some even without shoes. A priest comes up and says mass on that day."

"Without shoes! They must be mad. "

"They believe they are paying for what they have done wrong in their lives."

"I'll keep my shoes on."

21 **loose** [luːs] *lose* – 26 **to say mass** *eine Messe lesen*

"Me too, but just look out there. This is one reason why I love Ireland so much, Carl." They were looking out over Clew Bay.

"So many islands, Dad!"

5 "Yes, it is said there's an island for every day of the year down there."

"Fantastic. Really cool."

"It is, son. It's beautiful."

They were enjoying being together. His father 10 took him by the hand and led him to a rock, where they sat down.

"You're so quiet, Dad. What's wrong?"

"I don't know where to begin." He paused, was silent for a moment and then went on. "You 15 know your mother and I haven't been very happy together." Carl didn't answer. "Well, we've decided to live separately … for a while, at least, to see if we can find a new way."

Carl started crying. "Please don't, please, Dad. 20 You're not going to leave me, are you?"

"Listen to me, Carl. I love you. I'll never leave you, I promise."

Joe put his arms around him. He knew he was hurting his son, but he couldn't help it. He looked 25 at the crying teenager in his arms and his own tears flowed down his cheeks. Slowly Carl stopped crying. Joe took out a tissue and dried his son's eyes.

"We both love you very much. We've tried and tried – it just didn't work. Mum has gone to Spain 30 for a week with a friend and I'm here. We're both happier that way."

27 **tissue** [ˈtɪʃuː] soft paper to clean your nose or dry your eyes

Carl was silent. Joe explained that he'd never been happy in Germany. He'd gone there as a student to do some summer work and met Katrin. They fell in love and got married when he'd finished his studies.

"In my heart, I've always been Irish and Mum's heart is in Hamburg."

"But you're not going to leave Germany, are you, Dad?"

"No. I've got a small flat in Hamburg for us, and I'll be going back and forward to Ireland now, organizing English language courses for young Germans in Dublin. I got this new job two weeks ago and I'm really happy about it. I don't have to teach English any more."

"I want us always to be together, Dad."

"We will be, Carl. And with Mum as well, but in a different way."

They stood together looking out over the bay. When they got back down to the bottom of the mountain, Carl said he'd like to call his Mum on her mobile phone. After the call, they drove down the coast towards Achill Island where they would spend the next three days together.

Chapter 14

They came back from their trip on the Sunday afternoon.

"Only a few days until I leave. I'm flying on Wednesday morning," thought Carl.

5　When Carl didn't want to go to Dublin by car, Joe was surprised but didn't say anything. They had had a great time together in the last few days. They'd raced up and down Keel Strand till they were exhausted. Carl's Dad was still faster, but only just.

10　From Achill Head, you looked out across the wide Atlantic Ocean and when you turned inwards, the landscape was covered with white cottages facing the midday sun. It was all wonderful, except for 'the one thing'. They talked and talked and he rang his
15　Mum every day. He wanted to tell Liz and Shane all about it.

"Liz has no mother at all," he thought and that helped him.

"I'll take the afternoon train tomorrow, Dad."

20　"If you want, Carl. You're a big man now. Fifteen!"

"And nearly as tall as you. Just you wait."

Granddad and he walked to the hill a last time.

"Remember, you and your mother are very important to us. Never forget that. And I want you
25　to know that our night in the graveyard was one of the happiest nights in my whole life. Maybe one night you'll stand there with your grandson – I hope you do."

"Thank you, Granddad. I've learned so much
30　from you – things I'll never forget."

---

9 **exhausted** [ɪgˈzɔːstɪd] very tired

Shane was happy to see him. They talked everything through for an hour.

"Say goodbye to the team for me, I'll be back next year."

5 "And I'll try to get the money together to visit you. I'll write anyway."

"Don't forget."

The train was leaving at one o'clock. They all got together for a last goodbye at eleven. Carl felt loved 10 and happy. His Dad took him to the station.

"See you next week, pal."

"Sure, Dad."

It was strange being back in Dublin. In the train, he had read Liz's card again. "I'm so looking forward to 15 seeing her," he thought.

In the back of the car, Kate told him Liz would be around at eleven next day and they'd be going into the city together. She smiled and said she'd so much to do, she wouldn't be able to stay very long 20 with them. Carl smiled back.

Kate and he had a cool time that day just doing very little. They all went to bed early and got up at eight. Elaine and Philip were on late shifts, so they had a relaxed breakfast. He went with Kate to the 25 corner shop and was back at ten-thirty. He was so nervous about seeing Liz again. Then the doorbell rang.

"Get that, Carl," Kate shouted. He did. Liz looked brilliant in her cool colours. Her hair was shining 30 and her eyes were smiling. He'd put on his new jeans and a jacket he'd bought in Hamburg but hadn't worn before.

---

14 **to look forward to** *sich freuen auf* – 23 **to be on late shift** to start and finish work late in the day

"My goodness, but you look smart, Liz," Elaine said, staring. "Where's baby Liz gone to?"

"Will you listen to her, … my mother's funny … really funny, I tell you," cried Kate.

5 The three were laughing as they set off for the bus. At the corner of the South Circular Road, Kate said suddenly: "I'm awfully sorry, you two, but I've just thought of someplace very important where I've got to spend the day." And she was gone.

10 "We have the day to ourselves, Carl."

"Did you two plan this?"

"Never trust women, young man."

"After this I won't, but I'm happy not to this time."

They went back to Temple Bar and the Ha'penny 15 Bridge; they even took a bus out to Phoenix Park. "I'm buying the pizza tonight, Carl. I got extra hours in the shop, so I've got my own money. Yahoo!"

They got in a bit later than eight, but nobody said anything.

20 "How was it, Carl?"

"Fantastic. Just brilliant, Kate."

"I'll be asking Liz."

Carl knew he'd always be friends with Kate.

His mother met him at the airport and they had so 25 much to tell each other that it was very late before he got a chance to go to his room and write to Liz. He'd write to the others later.

The End

12 **to trust** *(ver-)trauen*

Gaelic football

Gaelic football is still the most popular game in Ireland. All thirty-two counties have a team and they play in the All-Ireland championship each year: The finals are played in Croke Park in Dublin. This is a beautiful stadium with about 70,000 seats. When the counties play against each other in championship games, lots of people attend.

Some say Gaelic football is like a mixture of Australian Rules and Rugby, but it is not quite as hard or as rough.

There are goalposts at either end of the field, as in soccer, but the goalposts go high into the air – about fifteen metres – and the crossbar is about as high as it is on a soccer pitch. The pitch is longer and wider than a soccer pitch.

There are fifteen players on a team. A player may catch the ball, or play it on the ground as you would in a game of soccer. Usually players try to catch the ball and kick it as a goalkeeper in soccer would. If a ball is kicked over the crossbar, it's a point. If it goes under the crossbar, it's a goal. One goal is equal to three points.

You are not allowed to pick the ball directly off the ground. You must get your foot under it and you cannot just run with the ball in your hands. You may kick it to yourself or bounce it on the ground while running. Kicking it to yourself is called a solo run. Good players can run very fast while doing a solo run with the ball.

It's a free kick for the other team if you run more than three or four steps without playing the ball in some way whether you bounce it, solo with it, pass it to another player or try to score a goal or point.

Each team has a goalkeeper, six defenders, two midfield players and six forwards.

Gaelic football goalposts

For further information on Gaelic football, visit the homepage: **www.gaa.ie**

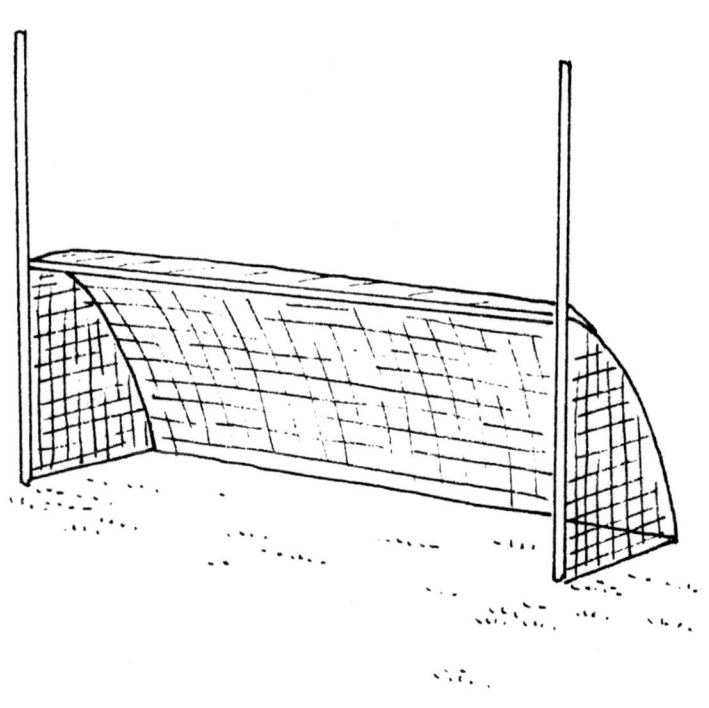

Map of Ireland

Activities

Before you read

1. Look at an atlas or an encyclopaedia.
   a) Where is Ireland in Europe?
   b) What is the capital of the Republic of Ireland?
   c) What sea separates Ireland and England?

2. Write a letter to a friend in Ireland, telling him / her you are coming to visit and asking questions about his / her home town and what there is to do there.

While reading

3. Carl keeps a diary when he's in Ireland. After reading each chapter, write the diary entry he makes.

4. Imagine you are Carl: write a letter to your mother in Hamburg telling her your father has told you about their problems and how you feel about it. Use words such as:

> bad • disappointed • unhappy • future •
> to live separately • to feel lonely • family •
> love • parents • children

After reading

5. What counties do you pass through on your way to Ballyhaunis? Name them. (Use the map on p. 59.)

6. Have you ever been to Ireland? How did you get there, where did you go and what did you like best? Compare your visit to Carl's journey. Write a short report.

7. When you have completed the book, choose two people from the story. Write down what you liked or didn't like about them. Use words such as:

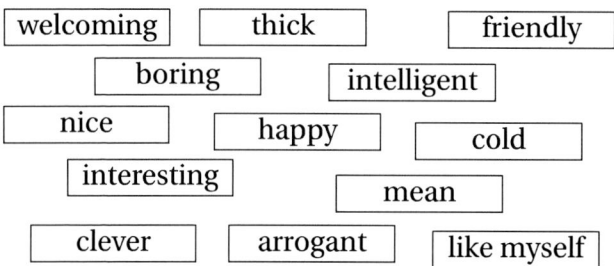

8. Do you believe Carl's Granddad when he talks about fairies? Do you believe in fairies or in things you can't see? Do you know any fairy tales from your area? If you do, tell the class one.

9. Word fields
   Below is a list of words from the story. Put them into three groups and find a heading for each group:

> fairy + soccer + little people + beer
> chocolate + score + mashed potatoes + tale
> shepherd's pie + crossbar + magic
> ring fort + ball + cornflakes + jersey + pitch
> poem + imagination + team + chips + tea
> player + fairy tree + kick + beans + goal
> sausage + bad luck

10. Why does Carl's Dad take him to the top of a mountain to tell him the sad news? Discuss first and then write.

11. What is the happiest or saddest part of the story for you? Why?

12. Look at the new words listed at the bottom of each page. Choose the ten words which you found most important or interesting. Write a new sentence with each of these words.

13. Are these facts correct?

	Yes	No
a) Kate, Liz and Carl walked into town.	☒	☐
b) The Burger Bar was near Trinity College.	☐	☐
c) There are skyscrapers in Temple Bar and it's modern.	☐	☒
d) The water in the river Liffey is very dirty.	☒	☐
e) There was fighting at the General Post Office in 1916.	☒	☐
f) Dublin has a Project Arts Centre, a castle and a cathedral.	☐	☐
g) The cathedral was named after King Arthur.	☐	☐
h) Shakespeare wrote about this famous cathedral.	☒	☐
i) Carl thinks Liz is really nice and very pretty.	☒	☐

14. In pairs: Try to explain to your partner – in English – how to play your favourite sport, e.g. soccer, tennis, volleyball, etc.

15. Look up the Gaelic Athletic Association on the internet. Would you like to play Gaelic football? Why or why not? (Girls also play, by the way.)

16. Use the internet to try and find some of the places mentioned in the story. For example: www.camvista.com

17. Complete the following text:
Gaelic football is still the most popular game in .... When the counties play against each other in the national championships, lots of .... attend. There are fifteen .... on a team. You can catch the ball, or play it on the ground. If a ball is put over the ...., it's a point. If it goes under the bar, it's a goal. One .... is equal to three points. There are goalposts at either end of the field, as in soccer, but they go high into the air and the crossbar is about as high as it is in soccer. You are not allowed to pick the ball up directly off the ground. You must get your foot under it and you cannot just run with the ball in your hands. You may kick it to yourself or .... it while running. It's a free .... for the other team if you run more than three or four steps without playing the ball in some way: you must either ...., ... or run with it. The field is longer and wider than a soccer field. A team consists of a ...., six defenders, two midfield players and six ....

Solutions

1. a) In the Atlantic Ocean, west of England and Wales
   b) Dublin
   c) The Irish Sea

5. You pass through Kildare, Meath, Westmeath and Roscommon, and then enter County Mayo.

13. The following answers are wrong: a), c), g), h).

17. The following words are missing: Ireland, people, players, crossbar, goal, bounce, kick, pass, shoot, goalkeeper, forwards.